DISCOVERING CANADA

The Loyal Refugees

ROBERT LIVESEY & A.G. SMITH

Stoddart Kids

TORONTO • NEW YORK

*We acknowledge for their financial support of our publishing program the
Government of Canada through the Book Publishing Industry Development
Program (BPIDP), the Canada Council, and the Ontario Arts Council.*

Published in Canada in 1999 by
Stoddart Kids,
a division of Stoddart Publishing Co. Limited
34 Lesmill Road
Toronto, Ontario M3B 2T6
Tel (416) 445-3333 Fax (416) 445-5967
E-mail Customer.Service@ccmailgw.genpub.com

Published in the United States in 1999 by
Stoddart Kids,
a division of Stoddart Publishing Co. Limited
180 Varick Street, 9th Floor
New York, New York 10014
Toll free 1-800-805-1083
E-mail gdsinc@genpub.com

Distributed in Canada by
General Distribution Services
325 Humber College Blvd.
Toronto, Ontario M9W 7C3
Tel (416) 213-1919 Fax (416) 213-1917
E-mail Customer.Service@ccmailgw.genpub.com

Distributed in the United States by
General Distribution Services
85 River Rock Drive, Suite 202
Buffalo, New York 14207
Toll free 1-800-805-1083
E-mail gdsinc@genpub.com

Canadian Cataloguing in Publication Data

Livesey, Robert, 1940 –
The loyal refugees

(Discovering Canada)
Includes index.
ISBN 0-7737-6043-1

I. United Empire loyalists – Juvenile literature. 2. American loyalists – Canada – Juvenile literature. 3. United States –
History – Revolution, 1775–1783 – Juvenile literature. 4. Canada – History – 1763–1791 – Juvenile literature. I. Smith, A.
G. (Albert Gray), 1945– . II. Title. III. Series: Livesey, Robert, 1940– .

FC426.L58 1999   j971.02'4   C98-932944-5
E277.L58 1999

Printed and bound in Canada

Dedicated with love to
Cousins Luke and Christine

A special thanks to David Moore; U.E.; Josie Hazen; the librarians at the Oakville Public Library; the Sheridan College Library; the University of Windsor Library; Horst Dresler; Sheila Dalton; and Kelly Jones.

Contents

Introduction

The American Revolution of 1775–83 created a new country, the United States of America, from the former Thirteen British Colonies. It also created a second country, Canada.

At the time of the revolution, one third of the people in the American colonies were loyal to the King of Britain, an equal number were in favour of armed revolution, and the last third were neutral.

The American Revolution was really the first American civil war. It was more like a family feud. It frequently turned neighbour against neighbour, brother against brother, and father against son. By the end of the conflict, more than 70,000 former residents of the Thirteen Colonies had left or lost their homes. Most travelled north to Canada, creating new cities and communities in what would become the colonies of New Brunswick, Nova Scotia, Prince Edward Island, Newfoundland, Lower Canada (Quebec), and Upper Canada (Ontario).

The displaced refugees felt the new, un-elected, rebel Continental Congress was a threat to their freedom. The Rebels had broken away violently from Britain with bloodshed and revolution; the Loyalists were disgusted with the open conflict, mob violence, and illegal actions. Although they remained loyal to Britain, they also demanded democratic and independent rights, but through peaceful evolution. Loyalists changed the nature of the Canadian wilderness and shaped the future personality of the Canadian people. They believed in law, order, and loyalty.

Events leading to the American Revolution

Ironically, when the inhabitants of the Thirteen Colonies revolted and declared independence in 1776 they already had more rights, liberty, and democracy than any other people in the world, including citizens in Britain.

The arrangement was that Britain protected her colonies from pirates and hostile enemies with her powerful army and navy, while the colonies supplied raw materials in return for manufactured goods from Britain.

Britain had let the colonies develop without too much interference or controls. There were British-appointed governors, often prominent colonists, who worked in cooperation with elected local assemblies of the people. However, with an ocean separating the two groups and a spirit of independence created by the frontier life on a new continent, a hostility grew between the mother country and her colonies.

Much like teenagers and parents today, the colonies objected to any British attempts to control them; while Britain felt it should curb the growing lack of respect for its rules and regulations. A series of events led to open conflict.

The Seven Years War (1756–1763)

During the Seven Years War between Great Britain and France, the American colonies fought loyally and bravely with Britain against the French. Every colony was loyal to the king. After the Battle on the Plains of Abraham*, where the British General Wolfe climbed the cliffs and captured Quebec City from General Montcalm in 1759, the British gained complete control of North America. In addition to the Thirteen 'American' Colonies

*see the third book in this Discovering Canada series, *New France*, for more information.

and the British colonies in the north such as Newfoundland, Nova Scotia, and St. David's Island (today Prince Edward Island), Britain now ruled Canada — where the people, at that time, spoke French and were mainly Roman Catholic.

Royal Proclamation (1763)

When King George III guaranteed native land rights in 1763, many colonists were angry. They felt that they were now prevented from expanding west across the continent. The Proclamation declared that the border between American settlers and native tribes would be the Appalachian Mountains. West of the mountains would be solely native territory.

The Stamp Act (1765)

This was one of many unpopular trade taxes imposed by the British government on its colonial citizens.

The Stamp Act declared that all business contracts had to be made on stamped paper purchased from British government officials. The British claimed they required the money to support a standing army, needed to defend the colonies and pay the debt from the war against France.

Most colonists agreed that the army was necessary but some insisted that they should vote to raise the tax, not have it imposed on them by Britain. Shouting "No taxation without representation!," violent mobs broke into the homes of the officials who were selling the stamps, destroying their property, and physically attacking them. Radical, illegal organizations were formed, calling themselves "Sons of Liberty." The act was withdrawn due to the protests. Some of the loyal colonists, although disapproving of the tax, became alarmed at the violence.

The Boston Massacre (1770)
More taxes on tea, glass, and other trade goods resulted in more resentment and mob violence. When a hostile crowd of Bostonians stoned a detachment of British soldiers, the troops fired on the crowd, killing some of their attackers. Rebel propaganda called it the Boston Massacre.

British ship *Gaspee* (1772)
A gang of Rhode Island smugglers, upset because the British naval schooner *Gaspee* was interrupting their illegal trade, captured and burned the vessel. Law and order was breaking down.

The Boston Tea Party (1773)
In December of 1773, an organized mob of protesters, angry about the tea tax, disguised themselves as Mohawk natives and attacked British ships in the Boston harbour. They threw 40,000 kg of tea into the water.

 Newspaper Stamp

 Document Stamp

March on Boston (1774)

There were no police forces in 1774. In an effort to restore law and order, Britain appointed General Thomas Gage, the military commander in America, as governor of Massachusetts. He sailed to the lawless city of Boston with a large army of soldiers. The Massachusetts assembly's right to choose its executive council was removed, town meetings were outlawed, and the port of Boston was closed, causing economic hardship.

Provincial Congresses (1774)

The political power struggle increased. Early in 1774, "committees of correspondence" were formed in every colony. They published propaganda and defied the elected colonial assemblies under the authority of the royal governors. Radicals created un-elected provincial congresses, to the dismay of the loyal citizens.

The Quebec Act (1774)

In 1774, the British passed the Quebec Act. It extended the borders of the colonies in Canada from the Labrador coast in the east, along the Ohio River in the south, to the Mississippi River in the west. To the north was Rupert's Land, the fur-trading territory of the Hudson's Bay Company. Canada, in 1774, included the present-day states of Michigan, Wisconsin, Illinois, Ohio, and Indiana.

The Quebec Act angered many of the citizens in the Thirteen Colonies to the south because it prevented them from expanding north and west. It also created a very unusual neighbour that spoke French and was officially Roman Catholic (unlike Britain or her other colonies in North America). In Canada, the priests kept their established legal rights to collect dues or taxes such as the *dîme* or tithe from the *habitants* (tenant farmers). The act decreed that Canada use the English Civil Law, but it kept the old French Civil Law.

Unlike the citizens of Britain and the Thirteen Colonies, the *habitants* of Canada had no elected assembly, only an appointed governor who chose his own council. The Quebec Act pleased the *seigneurs* (elite landlords) and the Catholic clergy who kept their traditional controls over the lives of the *habitants*, but it enraged the American colonists who believed it was a precedent that could threaten their elected representation.

War Breaks Out (1775)

In April of 1775, General Gage sent hundreds of troops from Boston to capture an illegal stock of weapons at Concord. The first shots were fired at Lexington and the British force was attacked by snipers along the road as they returned from Concord. Britain sent its three best generals to assist General Gage: the dashing "Handsome Jack" Burgoyne, the courageous

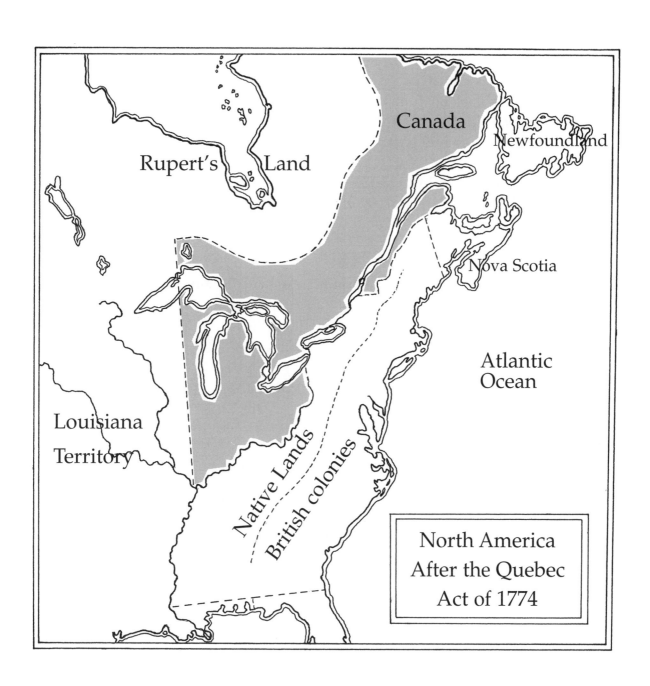

Rupert's Land

Canada

Newfoundland

Nova Scotia

Atlantic
Ocean

Louisiana
Territory

Native Lands

British colonies

North America
After the Quebec
Act of 1774

William Howe, and the shy but capable Henry Clinton. A bloody battle was fought at Bunker and Breed's Hill where the Rebels had gathered to threaten the city of Boston. Led by the daring William Howe, the British won but lost 40 percent of their troops. The rebel spirit was strengthened by the bloodbath of redcoats; loyal citizens were repulsed.

Colonial Army Created (1775)

The new Continental Congress created a Continental Army and placed George Washington in command.

Evacuation of Boston (1776)

Gage had failed to intimidate the rebel mobs with a show of force and thus was replaced as commander of the British troops by William Howe. In March of 1776, Howe, with 9,000 British soldiers and 1,000 loyal citizens who had gathered at Boston, assembled a large fleet of ships and sailed north to Halifax, in the British colony of Nova Scotia. The Thirteen Colonies were left without an armed British force; rebel armies quickly took advantage and control. Loyal citizens feared for their lives and property; many took up arms against their rebel neighbours.

American Declaration of Independence (1776)

To legitimize the revolution, Thomas Jefferson was asked to write the Declaration of Independence, and the Continental Congress ratified it on July 4, 1776. In the summer of 1776, the revolution seemed to be won.

1 *Attack on Canada*

Guy Carleton, John Burgoyne and Others

With the outbreak of war, the American rebels sent revolutionary armies north. An American army attacked Nova Scotia and an American privateer landed on St. David's Island (Prince Edward Island), taking the lieutenant-governor prisoner.

In 1775, George Washington sent an army of 2,000 to capture Montreal and Quebec City. Sir Guy Carleton, the governor of Canada, had only 750 troops to defend all of Canada because he had sent most of his British troops to Boston to support the show of force by General Gage.

Carleton had gained the trust of the French-Canadian *seigneurs* (landowners), clergy (priests), and *bourgeois* (businessmen) who remained loyal. The *habitants* (tenant farmers) were not so supportive. Some joined the rebel American army, but most remained neutral, ignoring British requests to form militia units and American invitations to revolt. At first, only about 100 volunteered to fight for Canada.

Ethan Allen's Vermont militia, the Green Mountain Boys, seized Fort Ticonderoga and Crown Point but the attack on Montreal failed and Allen was captured. An American army led by General Montgomery was delayed due to the strong defenses of Major Preston at St. John (St Jean) on the Richelieu but when the Americans captured Fort Chambly, St. John surrendered and Montreal was captured by the rebel forces.

Disguised as a *habitant* in homespun clothing and lying flat in a boat,

Carleton slipped past the American army surrounding Montreal in the middle of the night to escape to Quebec City. Montgomery followed Carlton to the Quebec Fortress, the last major fort in Canada still under British control. Another American army led by Benedict Arnold had marched through rugged wilderness for 46 days to reach Quebec City.

Montgomery sent a demand for surrender but Carleton burnt it without opening the envelope. Both Montgomery and Carleton had fought with Wolfe when he scaled the cliffs and captured Quebec in 1759.

On December 31, 1775 (New Year's Eve), the Americans attacked in the midst of a blinding snowstorm. General Montgomery, personally leading 350 men from the southeast, encountered barricades at an outpost at Cape Diamond defended by Captain Chabot with 30 Canadian militia and 15 English sailors. Despite the confusion and lack of visibility, Chabot calmly waited until the rebel army broke through a barricade (40 paces away) before he opened fire with large guns. The surprised attackers were devastated by the deadly blasts as red blood splattered on white snow. Montgomery was killed and his leaderless troops scattered into the raging storm.

At the same time, Benedict Arnold attacked from the northwest. He captured the first barricade but was wounded in the leg. When his troops attempted to take the second barricade they were driven back. Most of Arnold's men were taken prisoner.

One American general was killed, another wounded, 30 attackers were dead, and 450 captured; there were 7 Canadian defenders killed and 11 wounded. The Rebel attempt to capture Quebec City failed.

Arnold continued the siege of Quebec until a British fleet arrived in the spring led by the frigate *Surprise*, with over 9,000 professional troops commanded by "Handsome Jack" Burgoyne. Arnold quickly retreated into New York with the army of reinforcements in hot pursuit. By the summer

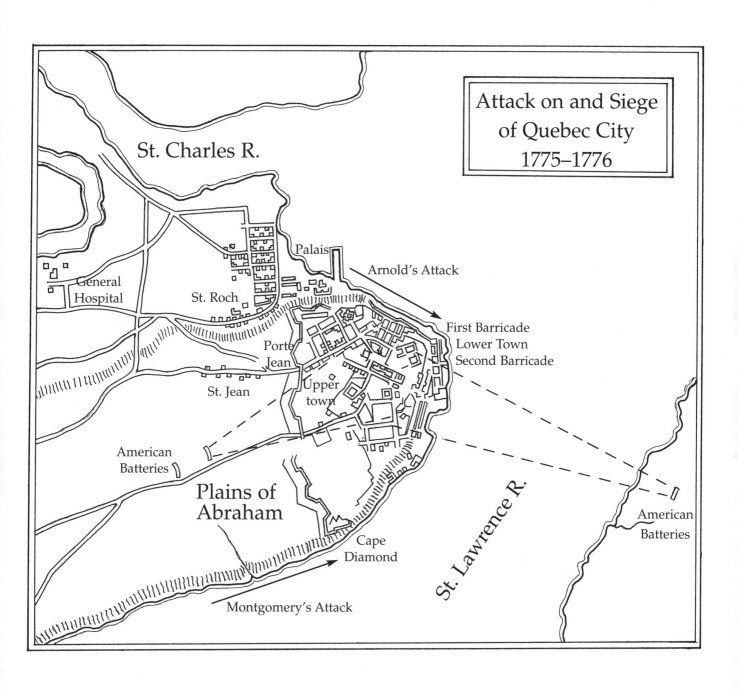

Attack on and Siege
of Quebec City
1775–1776

St. Charles R.

General
Hospital

St. Roch

Palais

Arnold's Attack

First Barricade
Lower Town
Second Barricade

Porte
Jean

Upper
town

St. Jean

American
Batteries

Plains of
Abraham

Cape
Diamond

St. Lawrence R.

American
Batteries

Montgomery's Attack

of 1776, Arnold's fleet on Lake Champlain was completely destroyed.

The Americans had hoped to find support for their revolution in the north but Canada, Nova Scotia, Prince Edward Island, and Newfoundland remained loyal to Britain and the American rebels were driven out.

Loyalist Hero or Rebel Traitor?

George Washington gave Benedict Arnold, one of the most trusted and heroic generals in the rebel army, the command of West Point, the powerful patriot fortification. He was shocked in 1780 to discover that his friend had changed his mind about the revolution and returned to the British side. A plot to hand West Point over to the British was discovered and prevented but Arnold, disgusted by the lack of support from the corrupt rebel congress, escaped and fought as a Loyalist for the rest of the war.

Young Wife

Peggy Shippen, a Loyalist, was 18 when she met 37-year-old Benedict Arnold. He arrived in Philadelphia in 1778, after the British forces evacuated it. She married the famous American Rebel the next year. She was aware that her husband was thinking about changing sides and she told friends she was responsible for encouraging him to do so.

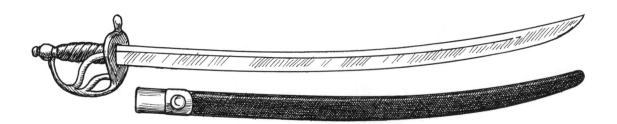

Sir Guy Carleton

Carleton Resigns

After his successful defense of Quebec and the arrival of reinforcements from Britain, Guy Carleton disagreed with the British secretary of war back in England and thus "Handsome Jack" Burgoyne was placed in command of the army in Canada. The insulted Guy Carleton asked to be replaced as governor. Frederick Haldimand, a Swiss-born soldier of fortune, was appointed as the new governor of Canada in 1777.

Criticized by the Press

In 1775, an article in the Quebec *Gazette* claimed:
> "If the country people . . . had chosen to follow the examples set by their seigneurs and by educated Canadians both in the towns and in the country, the rebels would never have dared to disturb our peace by invading this province."

Highland Loyalists

Many loyal Scottish Highlanders had settled in the colonies. Under the authority of General Gage at Boston, Allen Maclean formed a regiment of 1,000 Royal Highland Emigrants. Maclean was sent north to help defend Montreal and Quebec City where he became Guy Carleton's second-in-command. The defeat of the American armies attacking Quebec was largely due to the Highlanders. The defenders of Quebec were: 290 Highland Emigrants, 480 French Canadian Militia, 300 English Regulars, 24 sailors, and 30 Newfoundland carpenters used to build the barricades.

The Golden Dog

A tavern called The Golden Dog served as Allen Maclean's headquarters during the siege of Quebec. Maclean gathered support from the local people and even made the tavern owner's son, Samuel Prentiers, an officer in his regiment of Royal Highland Emigrants.

Damned by the Church

The Roman Catholic priests of Canada, led by Bishop Briand, supported the British defense and opposed any *habitants* who joined or aided the American invaders. One church proclamation read:

"All those who take up arms against the King are excluded from the way of salvation, unworthy to receive any sacrament, and unworthy of Christian burial if they die bearing arms."

Make a Model Cannon

See instructions on page 21.

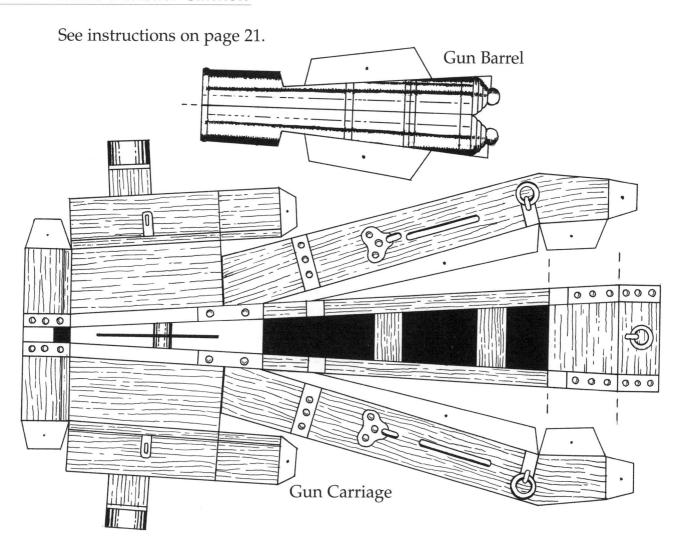

Gun Barrel

Gun Carriage

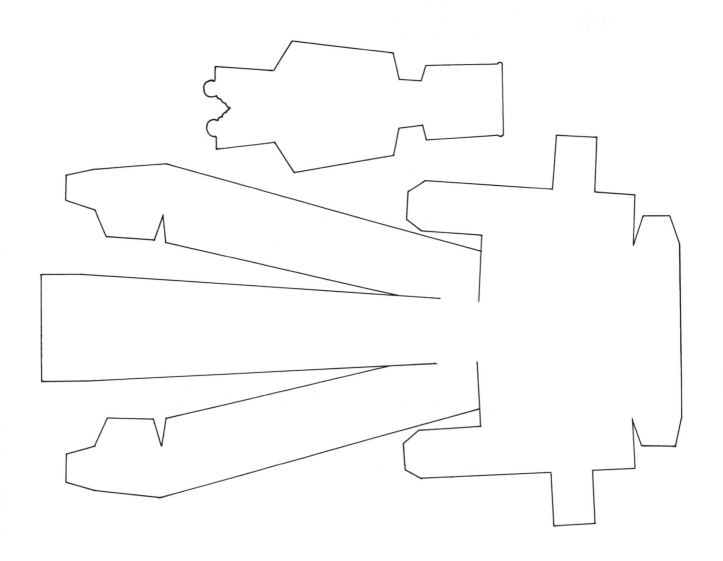

Inside of Wheels

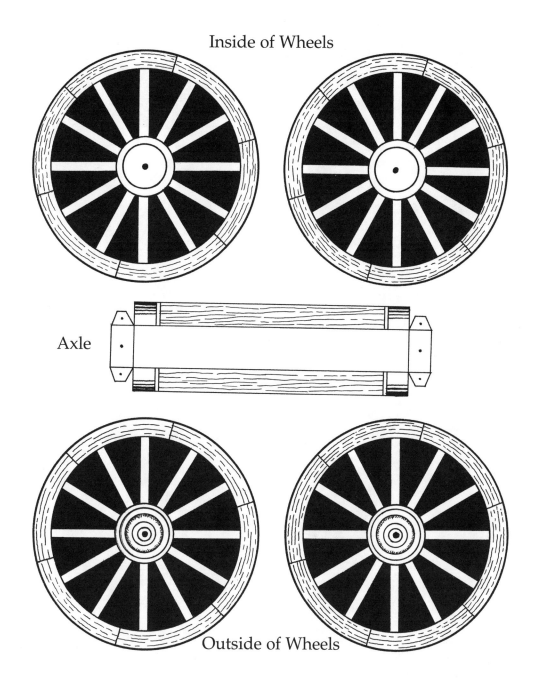

Axle

Outside of Wheels

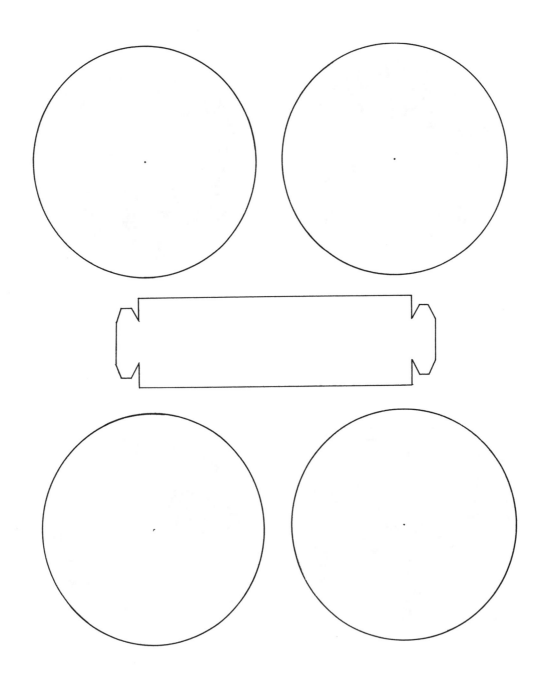

Make a Model Cannon

Both British and Rebel armies used cannons similar to this one during the "American War." Follow these instructions carefully to build your own.

What you need:

scissors   crayons or coloured pencils
white glue   scoring tool (like the point of a compass)

What to do:

1. Photocopy pages 17 and 19. Colour the parts before cutting them out. Do not colour tabs.

   Colouring suggestions: carriage and wheels — brown
   gun barrel — yellow (brass)   metal trim — black

2. Cut out wheels. Glue halves together. Apply glue to one half only.
3. Cut out the axle. Score along edges of tabs and fold them back. CAUTION: Apply glue only to the tabs. Do not use too much or it will seep through and spoil the paper.
4. Cut out and assemble the carriage. Be sure to cut a slot in the top of the carriage for the barrel.
5. Assemble the gun barrel.
6. Attach gun barrel to carriage.
7. Attach axle to carriage.
8. Attach wheels to axle.

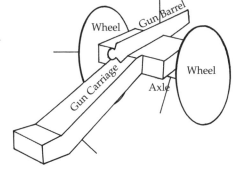

2 *Rebels and Loyalists*

William Howe, Henry Clinton and Others

When the first revolutionary Continental Congress met in 1775, there were representatives from all the Thirteen Colonies (except Georgia), but they didn't necessarily have the support of the majority in their colonies. With the creation of a Continental Army led by Washington and the Declaration of Independence written by Jefferson, emotional rivalry between the Rebels and Loyalists erupted in each of the colonies.

In some colonies, the Rebels, who called themselves patriots, clearly outnumbered the Loyalists; but in others, the Loyalists, called tories by their enemies, overshadowed the Rebels. Loyalists felt that their neighbours or friends who supported the rebellion were irrational traitors who were out of control. They believed their system of democratic government under the king was better than mob rule led by an un-elected congress. Rebels were convinced that Britain did not represent their interests and had no right to impose taxes or oppose colonial policies established by the new Continental Congress. The first American civil war became bloody and cruel as neighbours and relatives turned against one another.

Return to New York

In July of 1776, General William Howe returned to the Thirteen Colonies with an army of 26,000 experienced troops. He arrived at New York with a naval fleet commanded by his brother, Richard Howe.

George Washington's Continental Army of 16,000 inexperienced Rebels, poorly led and equipped, was no match for Howe's force which easily captured New York City. General Howe completed the capture of New York by taking the rebel stronghold of Fort Washington and chasing General Washington's troops deep into New Jersey. Loyal citizens cheered and welcomed the return of British authority as they formed militia units to support the British regulars. Howe's plan was to fight a major battle with the enemy army and destroy it, but the Rebels retreated and engaged in hit-and-run warfare with raids on the British outposts such as the attack at Trenton in 1776 on Christmas Eve. George Washington avoided William Howe's army as he spent the winter at Valley Forge.

Capture of Philadelphia
In 1777, Howe continued his strategy of attempting to engage and conquer Washington's forces. In the fall, he sailed with an army to Philadelphia, Pennsylvania, home of the rebel headquarters and Continental Congress. He successfully captured it from the Rebels after the Battle of Brandywine.

Saratoga
In 1777, "Handsome Jack" Burgoyne led an army of 7,000 from Montreal to invade the Thirteen Colonies via the Richelieu River and Lake Champlain. He was victorious against the American Rebels by recapturing Fort Ticonderoga, and then proceeded toward New York City.

At Saratoga, Burgoyne was surrounded by a rebel army led by General Gates and forced to sign a "convention," or agreement, to return with his army to Britain. After Burgoyne had surrendered his weapons, the Continental Congress broke the agreement and imprisoned the British troops until the end of the war. It was the invention of the prisoner-of-war

General
John Burgoyne

camp; up until this time in history, prisoners were kept only until they could be exchanged for prisoners captured by their opponent.

France Declares War

The rebel victory at Saratoga drastically changed the conflict. It encouraged France, Spain, and Holland to join the war against Britain (their traditional rival). Their combined fleets outnumbered Britain's. The colonial revolt became a world-wide conflict. Britain was threatened with invasion as were British colonies or bases throughout the world. Equally threatened was Britain's world trade, the source of its strength and power.

In 1778, Howe was replaced by Newfoundland-born General Henry Clinton whose new strategy was to confine the revolution in New York, New Jersey, and Pennsylvania.

Southern Offensive

Clinton's plan was to recapture the south, which had many loyalist supporters. In 1778, troops from Florida recovered Georgia. In 1779, a Continental Army at Charleston, South Carolina, was defeated. By 1780, most of Georgia, South and North Carolina were under British control.

The leader of the British forces in the south was General Cornwallis. In 1781, he moved north with an army of 4,000 on a long trek through the interior of North Carolina and arrived at Yorktown, Virginia, beside Chesapeake Bay on the Atlantic Ocean. He expected to meet the British fleet but was surprised to discover a French fleet and George Washington's Continental Army. There were 16,000 French and American troops outnumbering his force of 4,000. After more than a week of resistance, Cornwallis was finally forced to surrender in October 1781.

End of the War?

When General Cornwallis was forced to surrender to the French fleet and Continental Army at Yorktown in 1781, the British government decided to end the war, at any cost. The revolution in the colonies had escalated to a global conflict with France, Spain, and Holland. Britain wanted to return to peace and prosperous trading. It was willing to accept the independence of the United States of America, but peace negotiations took two years. In the meantime, Loyalists and Rebels continued to struggle for control of their homes, towns, communities, and colonies.

Saved by a Spider

On the run at the end of the American Revolution, William Schurman and his family were attempting to escape from rebel forces by hiding one night in a cave. As they slept, a spider was busy weaving its web across the entrance to the cave.

At dawn, they heard the approach of rebel soldiers. The loyalist family feared that their lives were lost but the Rebels saw the spider web and thought that no one could have entered the cave for, if they had, the web would have been broken. They passed by without searching the cave. The Schurman family eventually escaped successfully to Bedeque, Prince Edward Island.

Governor Arrested

When rebellion turned to open war, each of the British-appointed governors in the Thirteen Colonies dealt with Rebels in his own way. In Connecticut, Governor Trumbull decided to join the Rebels; in Rhode Island, Governor Wanton took no action and allowed the Rebels to do as they wished; in the southern colonies, most of the governors took shelter in forts or on ships; in New Jersey, Governor Franklin, illegitimate son of rebel leader Benjamin Franklin, tried to reason with the Rebels but they arrested him and sent him to jail in Connecticut.

Underground Prison

Rebel committees confiscated or destroyed the homes and property of their loyalist neighbours, forcing them into exile or sending them to prison. One of the most infamous prisons was Simsbury Mines where hundreds of loyalist prisoners were kept in abandoned mine shafts 21 metres under the ground. William Franklin, a former governor of New Jersey, was one of the loyalist prisoners sent to the cold caverns.

Cowboys and Skinners

Vengeance and atrocities were common on both sides of the bloody guerrilla war. In Westchester County, James De Lancey's Westchester Refugees were labeled "Cowboys" and "Cattle Rustlers," while the rebel vigilantes were called "Skinners" because they robbed or "skinned" the loyalist citizens.

Flora MacDonald

Many members of the huge and powerful MacDonald clan had settled throughout the Thirteen Colonies and remained loyal to Britain. In North Carolina, Flora MacDonald, her husband Allan, and their two grown sons fought openly against the Rebels. When their army was cut off and defeated by rebel forces, Allan and his sons were arrested and sent to prison, leaving Flora to cope on her own. Flora had become famous back in Scotland when she aided the Scottish Rebel Bonnie Prince Charlie.

29

Tarleton's Raiders

Some of the most devastating guerrilla raids took place in North and South Carolina as British officers such as Banastre Tarleton, leader of the Legion (known also as Tarleton's Raiders), terrorized rebel forces. Patrick Ferguson was in command of another militia, the American Riflemen. Other loyal southern forces were the South Carolina Regiment and the South Carolina Royalists.

Tarleton's Quarter

Tarleton gained a bloody reputation when he massacred rebel troops at the battle of Waxhaws in North Carolina in 1780. In October of the same year, Patrick Ferguson was killed in an encounter at King's Mountain. His troops asked for "quarter," which meant they wanted to surrender. Screaming "Tarleton's Quarter!," the rebel forces butchered over 200 of the Loyalists.

German "Mercenaries"

When the troop ships arrived from England to help General Howe recapture the Thirteen Colonies, they brought 26,000 professional soldiers. They included English, Irish, and Scottish regiments but the majority, 18,000, were German units hired in an arrangement with German nobility.

Rejoining the Empire?

Vermont dropped out of the war against Britain and her colonies in 1780 and threatened to rejoin the British Empire. Ethan Allen, who had captured Fort Ticonderoga and attacked Montreal in 1775, even invited displaced loyalist refugees to settle in Vermont. The reversal was due to a disagreement with the Continental Congress which was refusing to recognize Vermont as an independent state rather than a part of New York. Vermont's status was eventually recognized in 1792, many years after the war, and it became part of the new American republic again.

War Slogans

When people fight over different beliefs they frequently use slogans to express their attitudes. Slogans can show clearly the mood on both sides.

Rebel Slogan: *"A tory is a thing whose head is in England, and its body in America, and its neck ought to be stretched."*

Loyalist Slogan: *"We have traded one tyrant 3,000 miles away for 3,000 tyrants one mile away."*

Lynch Law

The term "lynch law," used to describe frontier justice based on mob rule rather than a legal court, originated in Virginia during the American Revolution. "Judge" Lynch was not a judge, but a colonel in the Virginia Militia. He liked to "hold court" in his home and "sentence" Loyalists to fines, prison, exile, or punishment. Crowds gathered to witness cruel "spectator sports" such as "tarring-and-feathering" which involved pouring boiling hot tar over the victim's naked body, then sprinkling feathers on top of the tar as an insult. It caused severe burns and, later, clumps of skin and hair would be torn off when trying to remove the tar. It could kill the person. "Rail-riding" meant tying a man to a sharp rail placed between his legs and then bouncing him on a painful ride through a town. It could ensure that he was no longer able to have children. Later the term "lynch law" included hangings or "lynchings" by enraged mobs.

Make a Gorget

See instructions on page 35.

Cut

Cut

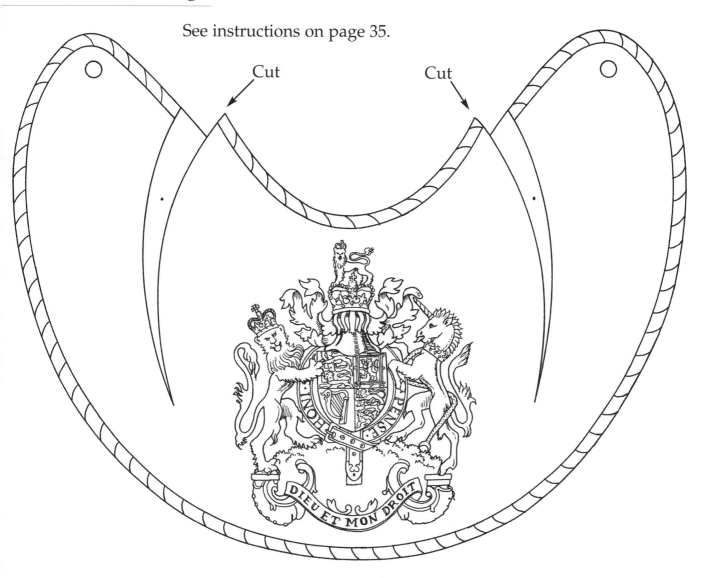

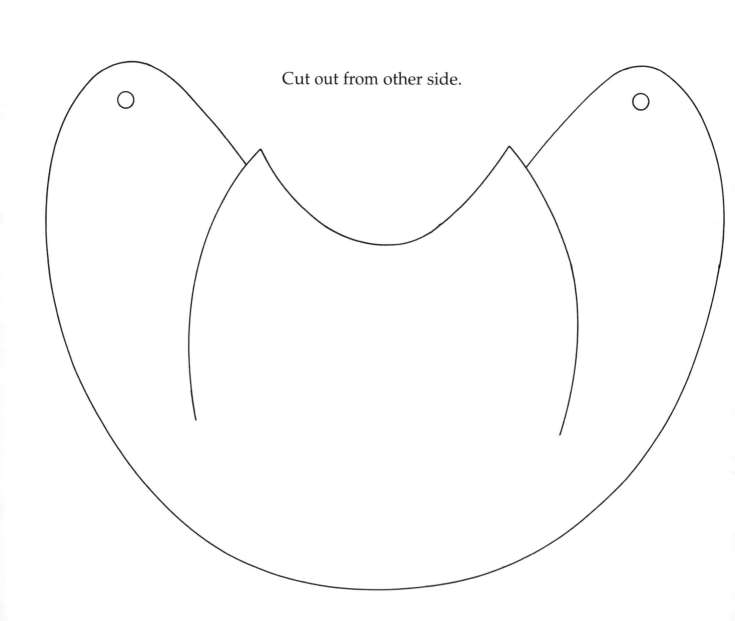
Cut out from other side.

Make a Gorget

A gorget was a ceremonial breastplate worn as a symbol of rank by military officers.

What you need:

scissors	crayons or coloured pencils
white glue	1/2 metre of twine or yarn

What to do:

1. Photocopy page 33. Colour the gorget yellow before cutting it out. Do not colour the tabs.

2. Glue the tabs beneath the folds on the sides. Apply glue only to the tabs. Do not apply too much glue or it will seep out and spoil the paper.

3. Punch holes in the corners and attach a piece of twine. You may now wear your gorget. (See the portrait of Joseph Brant on page 39.)

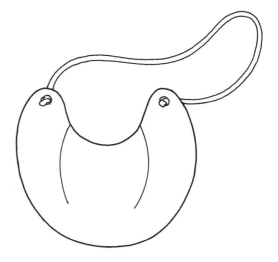

Joseph Brant, John Johnson, John Butler and Others

Like the settlers of the Thirteen Colonies, the native tribes were divided by the revolution. The Six Nations confederacy, called the Great Tree of Peace by the Iroquois, was torn apart. The Seneca, Mohawk, and Cayuga sided with the British; the Onondaga, Oneida, and Tuscaroras usually aided the Americans.

Joseph Brant, the Mohawk war chief, was a loyal supporter of the British. He had helped them defeat Pontiac, the Ottawa chief, who led a western uprising of Shawnees and Delawares in 1763.

The natives in the Mohawk Valley had been kept loyal to Britain by the popularity of Sir William Johnson, the Indian superintendent who was married to Joseph Brant's sister, Molly. When Sir William suddenly died of a stroke, his son John inherited his father's titles, but gave his cousin Colonel Guy Johnson the role of Indian superintendent. Joseph Brant became Colonel Guy Johnson's secretary of Indian affairs.

With the outbreak of hostility, both the Rebels and the Loyalists sought the support of the Six Nations. In 1774, Brant as well as Seneca war chiefs Old Smoke and Cornplanter were invited to Montreal by Sir Guy Carleton, the governor of Canada. Brant assured Carleton that 3,000 Mohawks would support the king.

Fort Stanwix (1777)

After a trip to England to meet King George, Brant returned to the Mohawk Valley in 1776. The opening battles of the revolution at Boston and Quebec were over, and Burgoyne advanced into New York in 1777. To aid Burgoyne's attack, Joseph Brant, war chief of the Mohawks, joined forces with Sir John Johnson's King's Royal Regiment of New York and Colonel John Butler's famous Butler's Rangers to try to capture Fort Stanwix. They surrounded the fort, and the siege became a long one.

Ambush at Oriskany (1777)

A rebel commander, General Herkimer, attempted to come to the rescue of Fort Stanwix, but Molly Brant sent a warning to the Loyalists who then ambushed his army. More than 400 of the rebel troops were killed, and General Herkimer died after his wounded leg was amputated.

Wyoming (1778)

Loyalist forces raided Wyoming in July of 1778. Many farmers' families were killed in an inhumane slaughter. Brant was not present during the raid but he was personally blamed by the Rebels for the outrage.

Cherry Valley

Brant was present at the raid on Cherry Valley although the commander of the force was John Butler's son Walter. Walter Butler had been badly treated in a rebel prison before he escaped to join his father's Rangers. The Senecas, seeking revenge for atrocities done to their women and children by the Rebels, conducted a bloody slaughter of settlers, sometimes including Loyalists as well as Rebels. More than 30 women and children were scalped and mutilated; most of the men were killed. Buildings and crops were

Joseph Brant

burnt. Brant personally prevented the Senecas from killing one loyalist woman but he arrived too late to stop the massacre. When John Butler heard of the atrocities, he was furious.

German Flatts
More raids by the Mohawks and the loyalist Rangers into the Susquehanna Valley of Pennsylvania and the Schoharie Valley of New York continued to terrorize the rebel settlers. The towns of Andrustown and German Flatts were ransacked and destroyed but, despite his reputation as a ruthless savage among the Rebels, Joseph Brant ensured that the loss of life was limited. He disapproved of senseless cruelty or murder.

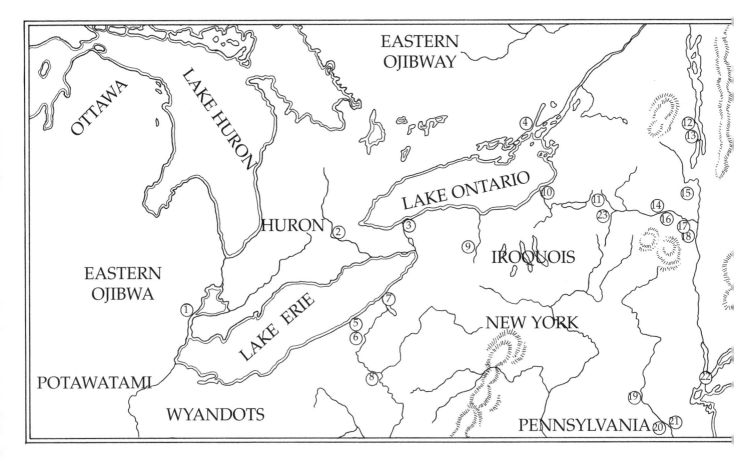

KEY TO MAP OF NATIVE LANDS AND REVOLUTION

1 Detroit
2 Brantford
3 Fort Niagara
4 Fort Frontenac
  (Kingston)
5 Fort Presque Isle
6 Fort Leboeuf
7 Westfield

8 Fort Venango
9 Wyoming
10 Oswego
11 Fort Stanwix
12 Crown Point
13 Ticonderoga
14 Fort Johnson
15 Saratoga

16 Cherry Valley
17 Fort Hunter
18 Albany
19 Easton
20 Philadelphia
21 Trenton
22 New York
23 German Flatt

Rebel Retaliation (1779)

In 1779, the rebel leaders sent General James Clinton with 5,000 soldiers to avenge the raids of 1778. Another rebel general, John Sullivan, led a second army from the west.

Loyalist Rangers and natives were forced to retreat as their homes and crops were destroyed. The Iroquois were a farming community; most lived in houses and towns like their white neighbours. Forty-one Iroquois towns were destroyed and ravaged. Productive farmland was burned. Men, women, and children were butchered.

Return of the Loyalists (1780)

In 1780, Brant's Rangers, John Johnson's Royal Yorkers, and Butler's Rangers struck back, attacking towns and settlements throughout New York until all rebel resistance was destroyed. By 1781, Rangers and natives were making raids south to Kentucky to free and rescue loyalist prisoners. At the Battle of Blue Licks, Butler ambushed rebel Daniel Boone's force, where Daniel's son died in his father's arms.

Iroquois War Club

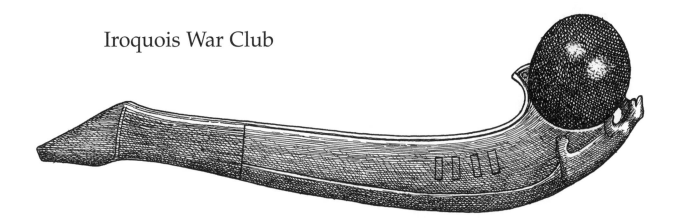

Colonel Guy Johnson (cousin of John Johnson) arranged to take Joseph Brant and Brant's cousin John Deseronto (Deserontyon) to England to meet King George. The native chiefs became instant celebrities and were showered with gifts. Brant received a gold watch and was made a full captain in the British Army.

Colonel Johnson knelt and kissed the hand of King George but when the king offered his hand to Brant, the chief pushed it aside, claiming that he would not kiss the hand of another man. The awkward moment passed when the gallant Brant offered to kiss the queen's hand instead. The natives felt they were loyal allies, not loyal subjects.

Powder Horn

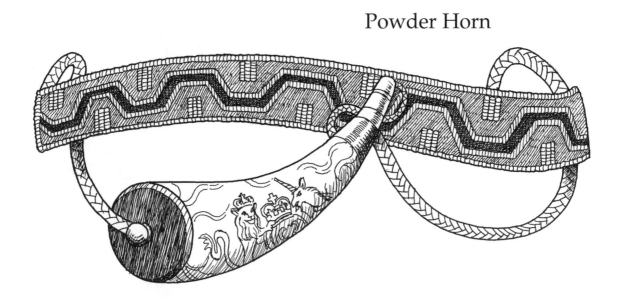

Tearful Chief

One of the American rebel soldiers present at Cherry Valley and a witness to the arrival of Joseph Brant after the gruesome massacre wrote of Brant's reaction:

> "(Brant) turned round and wept and then, recovering himself, told Butler he was going to make war against America but not to Murder and Butcher."

Attacked by Privateers

During their return voyage from Britain to North America in June of 1776, Joseph Brant and Deseronto saw a Yankee Privateer descending on their ship, the *Harriot*, crippled due to sea damage and sitting helplessly in the water. In England, the chiefs had each been given presents, including new rifles. They brought the weapons up on deck and began picking off the officers and men on the approaching rebel ship. After the natives shot five of the attackers, the enemy ship turned away and left them alone.

Battle ID

Today, soldiers wear ID tags when they go into battle to identify them if they are killed. In England, Joseph Brant purchased a gold ring and had both his white and native names (J. Brant–Thayendanegea) carved on it for identification in case he died in battle.

Women Leaders

Although no women could be elected or appointed to government (in fact, they had no voting rights) in Britain or the American colonies in 1776, that was not the case in the Mohawk nation. The Iroquois* had a matriarchal form of government where the women elected the council of *Sachems*, or "wise men," who appointed the war chiefs to fight the battles. Children took the family names of their mothers, not their fathers.

Before Molly Brant married the rich and powerful Irish landowner of the Mohawk Valley Sir William Johnson, she was just as influential in the Iroquois nation as he was in white society. Her power in the native tribe was a great asset to Sir William in his role as Indian agent. Molly gave Sir William two sons and six daughters. This was in addition to his six children from previous marriages; three with a Mohawk woman, and three with a German servant. The latter included his son John Johnson.

Native Communities

The tribes of the Iroquois confederacy were traditionally farmers, not nomadic hunters. At the time of the revolution, most Mohawk towns and farms were not very different from the white communities next to them.

The Mohawk dressed fashionably and lived in the same kind of houses as the white community. Joseph Brant enjoyed his English tea and was a devoted Christian.

* see the fifth book in this Discovering Canada series, *Native Peoples*, for more information about the native tribes and their customs.

Hot-Tempered Wives

Joseph Brant admired women who were strong and forceful. His first wife, Owaisa (Peggy), an Oneida woman, was known for her fiery temper. She and Brant had a son and a daughter before Owaisa died of tuberculosis. Brant's second wife was Owaisa's half-sister Onogala (Susanna), but within one year, she too died of tuberculosis.

In 1775, the year the American Revolution erupted, Brant married Catherine Croghan, whose father was Irish and mother the head woman of the Mohawks. She had an even hotter temper than Owaisa.

Escape from the Rebels

John Johnson was forced to leave his pregnant wife, Polly, and 15-month-old son, William, when he went to Montreal to command the Royal Yorkers. Rebels ravaged the Johnson house, arrested Polly, and took her to Albany where she was interrogated. After the birth of her new son, a black servant named Long helped Polly escape on a 225 km hike in the freezing winter snow to New York City, then occupied by the British. Crossing the broken ice on the Hudson River, Polly held her baby while Long carried young William as they jumped from ice block to ice block. She finally bribed a boatman to take her to Manhatten Island, but the baby died in her arms. Reunited with John, she spent the rest of the revolution at Lachine in Canada where she gave birth to other children.

Royal
Highland
Emigrant

Loyalist Units

There were four British Military Departments during the revolution and each had militia units of loyal volunteers. The Southern Department was in Florida, the Central Department was in New York City from 1776 to 1783, the Eastern (or North-Eastern) Department was in Nova Scotia, and the Northern Department was in Canada, as created by the Quebec Act of 1774.

Royal Highland Emigrants

They were commanded by Allen Maclean who recruited the loyal, kilted Scots from their homes in Canada and the Mohawk Valley of New York. They were sent to defend Montreal and Quebec City in 1775 and remained in border forts along the frontier throughout the revolution, protecting Canada from rebel invasion.

The King's
Royal
Regiment

The King's Royal Regiment (of New York)

This provincial unit was commanded and equipped by Sir John Johnson, a rich and powerful landowner from the Mohawk Valley. It was the largest of the provincial corps and also known as the Royal Yorkers or Royal Greens. Forced from their homes by Rebels, these displaced refugees from New York arrived by the hundreds in Montreal with their wives and children in 1776. Based in Canadian territory, they conducted guerrilla raids on the northern states from 1777 to 1782, burning rebel supplies and freeing captured Loyalists.

Indian Department

The native warriors were a powerful force that worked closely with the provincial units. John Johnson's cousin and brother-in-law, Guy Johnson, was the superintendent of Indian affairs, Northern District.

Butler's Rangers

Led by John Butler and his son Walter, the Rangers were a mysterious, mobile force. In summer, they used canoes or followed wilderness trails. In winter, they travelled by sleigh or snowshoe. Dressed in comfortable woodland clothing and carrying rifles, tomahawks, and scalping knives, they were like modern-day commandos; attacking, burning, and then disappearing back into the dark forests. They worked closely with their native allies.

Mohawks

Commanded by Joseph Brant, the Mohawks and Brant's Rangers fought with Butler's Rangers and John Johnson's Royal Yorkers against the rebels, threatening their traditional territory in the Mohawk Valley of New York. Over 300 warriors and 200 women and children took shelter at Montreal; others fled to the protection of Fort Niagara.

Butler's Ranger

48

The King's Rangers

This Loyalist unit of colourful frontiersmen with feathers in their hats was established at New York City as part of the Central Department in 1779. Its legendary leader, Robert Rogers from New Hampshire, had been a folk hero in the Seven Years War. It was quartered at Fort St. Johns (St Jean) in Canada. Robert's brother James later took command. The King's Rangers sometimes acted as secret service agents on scouting missions into rebel territory.

The Loyal Rangers (of Vermont)

The three Jessup brothers — Edward, Ebenezer, and Joseph — travelled north to Canada in 1776 with a small army of loyalist refugees. Commanded by Major Edward Jessup and formed in 1781, the Loyal Rangers were made up of two earlier corps that had joined General Burgoyne's invasion of New York in 1777: **The King's Loyal Americans**, led by Edward's brother, Ebenezer Jessup; and **The Queen's Loyal Rangers**, led by John Peters of Connecticut.

King's
Ranger

Play Capture the Flag

What You Need:
A large field or playground
Two flags on small lightweight poles
Armbands of two colours for members of each team

Object:
To capture the flag of the opposing team while protecting your own flag from capture.

What to Do:
1. Lay out the field according to the diagram.
2. Choose a referee (a teacher or group leader).
3. Divide yourselves into two teams of eight or more players.

The Rules for Play:
1. Any player found in the enemy's territory may be captured by being tagged with two hands and yelling "caught." They are then placed in the guard house.

2. Guards must not stand closer than 10 metres from the flag. They may follow the enemy into the 10-metre zone.

3. A prisoner may be freed by a member of their team crossing the line and touching them while they are in the guard house. Both the prisoner and the rescuer are allowed to return to their own territories.

4. If a raider with the opposing teams' flag is caught before reaching his or her home territory, the flag is set up at the point where it was rescued and the game continues.

5. If neither side captures the enemy's flag with an agreed upon time (one hour), the referee ends the game by blowing a whistle. The game is won by the team that has the most prisoners.

To Begin the Game:
The two teams meet at the centre line, each team in its own territory. The referee explains the rules. The referee blows a whistle once. The teams return to their flag bases. The referee blows the whistle a second time and the play begins.

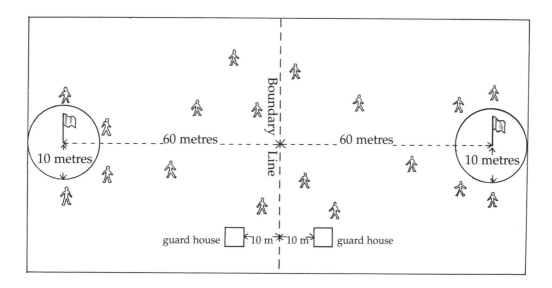

4 *Refugees in Exile*

Frederick Haldimand, John Parr and Others

At the Peace of Paris in 1783, American independence was accepted and all American territory defended by British Loyalists during the revolution was given to the Rebels. The war was over but the conflict between the colonists who had supported Britain and the victorious Rebels was still unresolved. The persecution of the Loyalists increased.

Lands, farms, homes, livestock, furniture, and clothing were destroyed, looted, or stolen. Men, women, and children were beaten, tortured, tarred-and-feathered, driven out of town, hanged, or shot by the Rebels. In some cases, angry mobs attacked the Loyalists; in others, "patriot committees" confiscated their homes and property, giving the assets to fellow rebel supporters. But many strong-minded Loyalists preferred exile to swearing allegiance to the new country.

Return of Carleton

Sir Guy Carleton, the former governor of Canada who had defended Montreal and Quebec in the early years of the war, was appointed the new commander-in-chief of the British forces in North America, replacing General Clinton. He had the difficult task of turning over the Thirteen Colonies to the Rebels while ensuring the safety and relocation of about 70,000 loyal British citizens. A mass migration began.

Most of the loyal refugees headed north where they built new homes and towns in the Canadian wilderness. Their great numbers and strong sense of duty, honour, and principle established the personality of the new communities that they moved into or created.

In the south, the inhabitants of the loyalist stronghold of Savannah, Georgia, were shocked to learn that all British troops were to be evacuated. More than 7,500 citizens had to abandon their city. East and West Florida, which had never been rebel territory, were given to Spain, forcing the dismayed Loyalists to relocate. More than half the refugees in the south were black Loyalists or black slaves owned by white Loyalists. Many slave owners relocated to plantations in the West Indies with their workers, but free blacks or escaping slaves preferred to sail for Nova Scotia. Guy Carleton refused the Rebel demands to return escaped slaves.

A huge population of over 35,000 Loyalists that had gathered at or around New York City had to be evacuated by Carleton before he withdrew his troops. He assembled a fleet of 183 ships, many of which would return several times for more passengers in the summer and fall of 1783. The ships travelled in groups of a dozen or more to protect themselves from the vicious American privateers that were hovering like vultures out on the ocean, waiting to kill and rob the evacuating refugees.

The first group sailed in the fall of 1782 for Port Roseway on the St. John's River. About 35,000 went to Nova Scotia in the summer of 1783. By October, all of the civilians had sailed and Carleton began removing his troops. In November, the last of the soldiers left New York.

The one to two week trip from New York to Halifax was a dangerous and unpleasant experience. The crowded vessels, often ridden with diseases such as measles and smallpox, had to cross the turbulent Bay of Fundy.

In September of 1783, the *Martha* smashed on rocks off Cape Sable Island. The 115 men, women, and children who died in the shipwreck were Maryland Loyalists and James De Lancey's Westchester Refugees.

Nova Scotia

In 1782, the new governor of Nova Scotia, an ex-soldier named John Parr, was faced with a massive flood of refugees who had to be cared for, equipped with provisions, given land, and aided in relocating. There were only 12,000 settlers in Nova Scotia before the arrival of 35,000 refugees. Twenty thousand of those refugees arrived in peninsular Nova Scotia and another 15,000 in continental Nova Scotia (today New Brunswick).

Before the arrival of the refugees, Halifax, the headquarters for the British fleet in North America, was more of a military post than a settlement. Every loyalist refugee was promised a generous land grant of 40 hectares, with 20 more hectares for each member of the family, plus more land if the man had held military or senior government positions. Food, lumber, equipment, and seed had to be distributed to the new arrivals. The new settlers became not only farmers but business people, involved in logging, shipping, and fishing.

LEGEND

1. The MacDonald Clan including Flora and Allan MacDonald from North Carolina (1778) (Windsor, Nova Scotia)

2. The British Legion "Tarleton's Raiders," from North and South Carolina (1783) (Port Mouton, Nova Scotia)

3. The Black Pioneers Thousands of free blacks and escaped slaves (Birchtown, Nova Scotia, and other towns)

4. New York Refugees, (first fleet May 4, 1783) (Port Roseway — new town — later Shelburne)

5. Loyalists from Albany, New York, led by Abraham Cuyler (Cape Breton Island)

6. Rhode Island Loyalists settled on P.E.I.

7. New York Loyalists founded the town of Summerside, P.E.I.

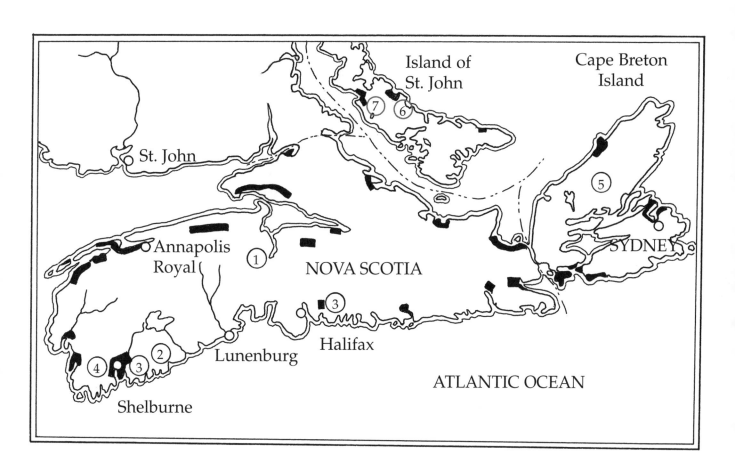

Island of
St. John

Cape Breton
Island

St. John

⑦ ⑥

⑤

Annapolis
Royal

① NOVA SCOTIA

SYDNEY

③

Halifax

Lunenburg

② ③

④ ③

ATLANTIC OCEAN

Shelburne

New Brunswick

Fort Howe at the mouth of the St John River was a small, quiet outpost until the summer of 1783 when 15,000 refugees arrived in wave after wave from the New York City evacuation. Frantic officials had to assign land grants to the refugees who were desperate to plant a crop before winter set in. The trading city of St. John was created. Other refugees travelled farther west to Passamaquoddy Bay.

The migration of large numbers of Scottish Loyalists from the Thirteen Colonies into Nova Scotia brought new problems. They were loyal to Britain but accustomed to elected assemblies and just as devoted to creating new rights for their colony as the American Rebels. They would not, however, resort to armed rebellion.

The Quebec Act did not allow for elected democratic government, and within months the new arrivals were demanding their own colony, independent from Nova Scotia and Governor Parr in Halifax. They went directly to the British government. The result was that, within a year, by June of 1784, the colony of New Brunswick was created from continental Nova Scotia. Thomas Carleton, brother of Guy Carleton, became its first governor. When Governor Parr died in 1791, loyalist refugee John Wentworth, the deposed governor of New Hampshire, replaced him.

LEGEND

1. Westchester Refugees James De Lancey's First Battalion of Westchester Refugees from upstate New York (1783)

2. King's American Regiment from North and South Carolina, commanded by Edmund Fanning

3. King's American Dragoons

4. New Jersey Loyalists (Saint John, New Brunswick)

5. Prince of Wales Regiment

6. Pennsylvania Loyalists

7. Queen's Rangers

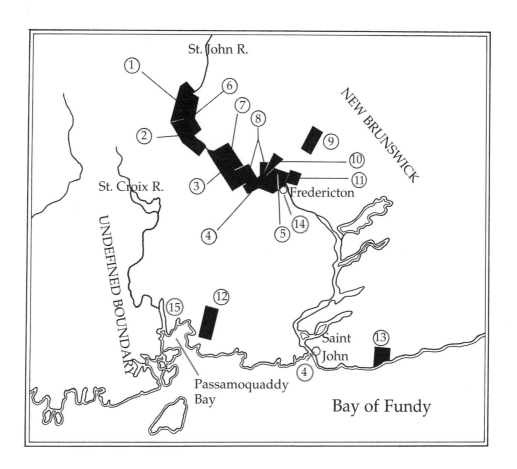

St. John R.

NEW BRUNSWICK

St. Croix R.

UNDEFINED BOUNDARY

Fredericton

Passamoquaddy Bay

Saint John

Bay of Fundy

8. Guides and Pioneers

9. 42nd Regiment

10. New York Volunteers

11. Maryland Loyalists

12. Royal Fencible Americans

13. Orange Rangers

14. **The King's Americans** and other provincial corps (the Saint John River Valley of New Brunswick and at St. Anne, later renamed Fredericton)

15. **Penobscot Loyalists from Maine** Crossed Passamaquoddy Bay (1783) (St. Andrews, New Brunswick)

Cape Breton Island

Cape Breton, with almost no settlers, was overrun by the flood of loyalist arrivals and, led by Abraham Cuyler from Albany, New York, it also split from Nova Scotia in 1784 to became a new colony*. That same year, about 400 refugee Loyalists arrived from New York and 140 came via Quebec City. By 1785, elections in New Brunswick and Cape Breton had created colonial legislatures controlled by the new refugees.

Prince Edward Island

Before 1783, the Island of St. John was independent and almost uninhabited, controlled by rich property owners. When 800 refugees arrived from New York, the town of Summerside was created and the Island of St. John was re-named Prince Edward Island.

Some loyalists went to Newfoundland as well, but not in the same drastic numbers that re-shaped the other British colonies in the north.

Lower Canada

Frederick Haldimand, Canada's governor between 1777 and 1786, was a Swiss-born soldier-of-fortune. His task, like Governor Parr's in Nova Scotia, was to cope with thousands of loyal refugees arriving from the south. His problems were greater because the new arrivals were English-speaking Protestants hoping to settle in a French-speaking, Catholic colony. Some sailed to the Gaspé Peninsula to create English-speaking towns at Chaleur Bay and Gaspé.

Allen Maclean's Scottish Highlanders from the Mohawk Valley had been in Montreal and Quebec since 1775, when they had been greatly

*Cape Breton later rejoined Nova Scotia to become part of that province

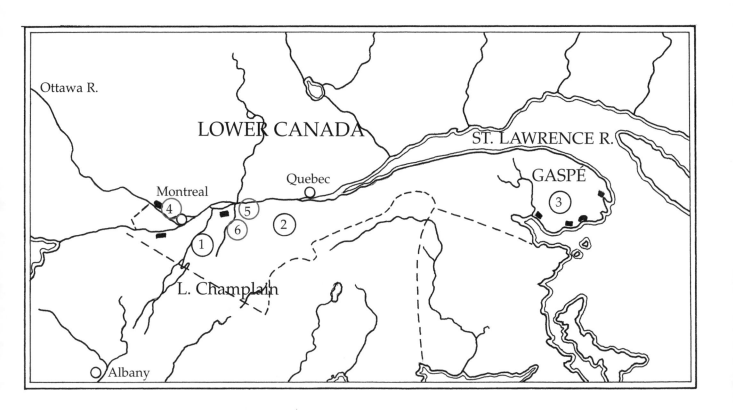

LEGEND

1. Jessup's Loyal Rangers (of Vermont) Vermont and Connecticut Loyalists commanded by Edward Jessup and Robert Leake (Settled in the Eastern Townships of Quebec) Sorel, Chambly and St. John (St. Jean)

2. New York City Evacuation (1783) Backwoods farmers from New York 1300 refugees to Lower Canada

3. New York Loyalists English-speaking towns created at (New Carlisle, Chaleur Bay and Gaspé in the Gaspé Peninsula)

4. European born Scots and Germans (Montreal)

5. Loyalists from New Hampshire, New Jersey, Pennsylvania

6. The King's Rangers Led by Robert and James Rogers.

responsible for defeating the invading rebel armies. From 1776 to 1783, "provincial troops" from loyalist units had taken shelter and established headquarters in Canada. They successfully protected the Canadian borders from rebels as they raided the American Colonies south of the border. About 10,000 loyalist soldiers and their families had moved north into Lower Canada by the end of the war.

The Peace Treaty gave to the Rebels all the forts successfully defended

by the loyalist units, forts such as Oswego, Niagara, Detroit, and Michili-mackinac. Haldimand was especially shocked and concerned when he learned that the British had also given the traditional Iroquois homelands in the Mohawk Valley to the Rebels.

Haldimand saw the huge wilderness known as the "Upper Country" as the solution to his problems and as a potential home for the thousands of English-speaking refugees. It angered Haldimand when Vermont Loyalists from Jessup's Rangers settled in the border country east of Lake Champlain, in the garrison towns of Sorel, Chambly, and St. John (St. Jean) on the Richelieu River. In 1791, after Haldimand retired, the English settlements were finally recognized as the Eastern Townships.

Upper Canada

The vast and fertile lands of present-day Ontario were opened to the English-speaking Loyalists migrating north from the Thirteen Colonies. It became the first inland colony.

When the loyalist regiments that had fought in the rebellion were officially disbanded in 1784, their members were given land grants and supplies by the British government to create new homes, farms, and towns in the Canadian wilderness. All settlers had to swear allegiance to the king but no one had to pay taxes, because taxes had been a major cause of the American rebellion.

In 1784, Haldimand retired to Britain and Guy Carleton returned to replace him as governor of Canada. The man who had overseen the evacuation of the refugees was now eager to help them re-locate.

The Front

"The Front" was the term used to describe the northern shore of the St. Lawrence River and Lake Ontario. It became the most important settlement area. Special multi-oared bateau were built below the rapids at Lachine to take the refugee families along the St. Lawrence into Upper Canada. The boats were 8 to 12 metres long, pointed at both ends, equipped with oars, poles, and sails. The 1.8 tonne vessels could survive in one metre of water, enabling them to traverse the treacherous rapids. The Loyalists had been friends and neighbours before the revolution and fought together during it. In Canada, they created communities along The Front, settling by regiment and vowing to defend their new homes.

Eight Royal Townships were created from Coteau-du-Lac to the present site of Brockville, and eight Cataraqui Townships from Kingston to the Bay of Quinte. By 1784, Loyalists were well established along The Front and building the new towns of Brockville, Cataraqui (Kingston), New Johnstown (Cornwall), and Prescott. The last three Cataraqui Townships were settled after 1790 by Late Loyalists (those loyal during the war who tried to remain in their homes afterwards without success). Disgusted with their treatment by the Rebels, they eventually moved north to obtain British land grants.

Niagara Peninsula

Butler's Rangers settled at Niagara-on-the-Lake where they had built a barrack in 1778. Some travelled to the other end of Lake Erie, near Fort Detroit (Windsor). After 1791, 30,000 Late Loyalists arrived.

LEGEND

1. The King's Royal Regiment (of New York)
Commanded by Sir John Johnson
Royal Townships #1–5
#1 Catholic Highlanders
#2 Scottish Presbyterians
#3 German Calvinists
#4 German Lutherans
#5 Anglicans
New Johnstown (Cornwall)
and at Cataraqui Township #4
Cataraqui (Kingston)
2. Butler's Rangers
Commanded by John Butler
Niagara-on-the-Lake,
also near Fort Detroit, Windsor
3. Mohawks
Commanded by Joseph Brant.
Brantford settlement on the Grand River (1784)
Commanded by Deseronto
Bay of Quinte settlement (1784)
4. Jessup's Loyal Rangers (of Vermont)
Royal Townships #6–8
Cataraqui Township #2
Vermont and Connecticut Loyalists
commanded by Edward Jessup
Brockville and Prescott.
5. Associated Loyalists of New York
Cataraqui Township #1
Led by Captain Michael Gross (1784).
6. King's Rangers
Cataraqui Township #3
Led by Major James Rodgers
7. British and German Regulars
Cataraqui Township #5
8. Late Loyalists (after 1792)
Cataraqui Townships (#6, #7, #8)
Belleville settled in 1790
9. New Jersey Volunteers
Commanded by Capt. Sam Ryerse (Ryerson)
Cataraqui Townships (#6, #7, #8)

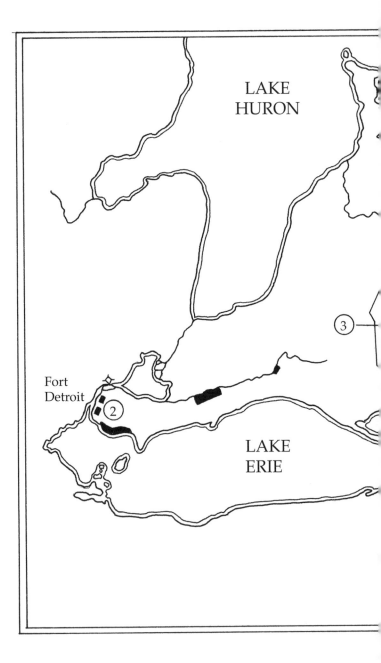

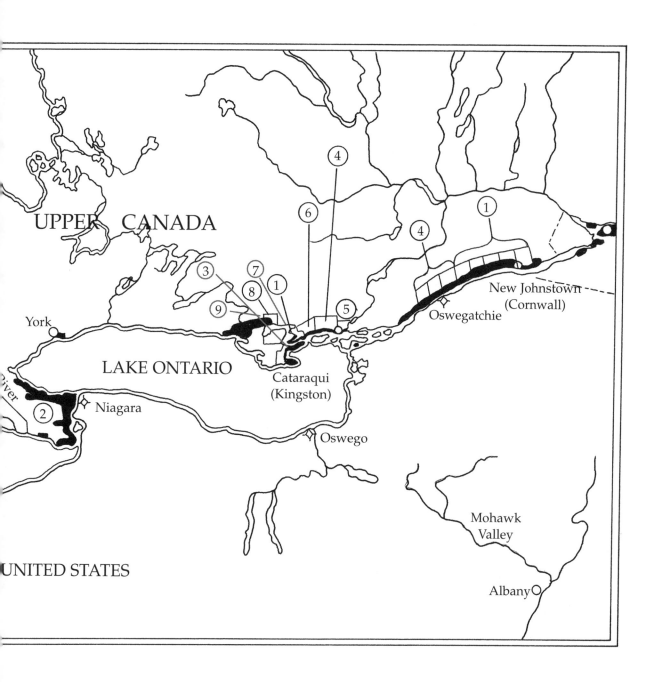

UPPER CANADA

York

LAKE ONTARIO

Niagara

Oswego

Cataraqui
(Kingston)

Oswegatchie

New Johnstown
(Cornwall)

Mohawk
Valley

Albany

UNITED STATES

The loyal Native Peoples' lands were not secured at the Treaty of Paris. Joseph Brant travelled to Quebec City, seeking help from Governor Haldimand to remedy this matter. Like the Loyalists forced from their homes in America, he received money, supplies, and land for his people.

Joseph Brant was given a land grant 10 kilometres wide along the Grand River in Upper Canada, from its source to its mouth on Lake Erie. The famous chief created a new settlement at Brantford where he built a town with a church, school, and council chamber. More than 1,500 natives, the largest group of refugees in 1784, followed Joseph Brant to relocate in Canada. They claimed to be loyal allies, not loyal citizens of the king. In 1784, Brant's cousin John Deseronto and 300 Mohawks settled on a land grant around the Bay of Quinte where a town is still named after him.

United Empire Loyalists

Colonists who fought for Britain during the revolution and lost their property to the Rebels were given the privilege of placing the letters "U.E." after their names. The letters stood for "Unity of the Empire." These settlers became known as the United Empire Loyalists. Today, their descendants also have the right to place "U.E." after their names.

Cataraqui Settlement

Late Loyalists

From the late 1780s to the War of 1812, a new wave of more than 30,000 immigrants from the USA poured into Upper and Lower Canada and New Brunswick. Some had been unable to leave during the revolution. Others were reformed rebels disillusioned with the new system of government in the USA which collapsed in 1790 and had to be replaced. Still others came for the free land grants. Their loyalty and motives were far more questionable than the original Loyalists.

Canada Divided

Sir Guy Carleton was given the title of Lord Dorchester, and returned as governor of Canada. He had fought bravely during the war and at its conclusion was commander-in-chief of the British Army in North America.

He respected the Loyalists who had moved into Canada after the revolution and wanted to give them the democratic rights and local self-government which they had had in the Thirteen Colonies. In 1791, he convinced the British government to pass the Constitutional Act. It created Upper Canada (now Ontario) and Lower Canada (now Quebec). This allowed the new lieutenant governor of Upper Canada, John Graves Simcoe, to have an elected parliament. At the same time, it maintained the traditional control of the *seigneurs* and clergy over the *habitants* in Lower Canada.

Largest Town

From 1783 to 1784, Port Roseway on the south shore of Nova Scotia was the largest town in British North America. In May of 1783, 4,000 civilian Loyalists arrived; by 1783, the population had reached 10,000. The new citizens renamed their town Shelburne. Later, Halifax would prosper and grow while Shelburne shrank.

Unpopular Refugee

Benedict Arnold, the famous American general who had changed sides during the revolution, became a refugee. He moved his wife, children, and sister to Saint John, New Brunswick, in 1787 but by 1791, the general had become so unpopular in the loyalist settlement that a violent mob attacked his house and burned an effigy with the word "traitor" on it. This led Arnold to sell off his belongings and sail, with his family, to Britain.

Match the Job

If you were deciding what job you wished to have in 1783, the choices would be very different than today. Can you match the following jobs to the correct descriptions?

What You Need:

a pen or pencil
a blank piece of paper

Do not write in this book!

1. mason
2. cooper
3. caulker
4. chimney sweep
5. blacksmith
6. miller
7. wheelwright
8. sawyer
9. domestic
10. liveryman

What To Do:

1. Write the numbers of the jobs from 1 to 10 down the left-hand side of the paper.
2. Place the letter of the job description on the opposite page beside the number of the matching job.

What I do:

a. I hammer and shape iron.

b. I stop up the seams of a ship with oakum and melted pitch.

c. I clear away soot.

d. I make or repair barrels, casks, or pails.

e. I am a household servant.

f. I keep horses and work in a stable.

g. I cut and carve stone and brick.

h. I grind corn and other grains into flour.

i. I cut wood or timber.

j. I make or repair circular frames used to facilitate motion and move objects.

The answers are on page 88.

5 *Black Loyalists*

Thomas Peters, Henry Washington and Others

George Washington, elected member of the Virginia legislature, is famous for his military achievements in the American Revolution against British authority and for becoming the first president of the United States of America. Most agree that he symbolized victory for freedom and democracy; few are aware that he owned hundreds of slaves who laboured on his prosperous Mount Vernon plantation.

In 1770, 40 percent of the people in Virginia were black slaves; one sixth of the population in all the Colonies was black. The American Revolution won independence and democracy only for the rich land owners who were white and male. Democratic rights for non-landowners (the poor), women, and blacks would evolve later in American history.

Freedom

In 1775, Lord Dunmore, governor of Virginia, freed all Rebels' slaves, but not Loyalists' slaves. About 300 former rebel slaves formed a regiment under the governor's name. They wore the slogan "Liberty to Slaves" across their chests. The same offer to be freed was later made to slaves throughout the colonies by Sir Henry Clinton, the commander-in-chief of the British forces. During and after the American Revolution, the British continued to offer freedom to Rebels' slaves. Another military unit of black Loyalists was the Black Pioneers.

Exodus to Canada

In 1783, 3,500 black Loyalists fled to Nova Scotia and New Brunswick, including some of George Washington's escaped slaves. One, named after his former owner, was Henry Washington. In Canada, black Loyalists were promised land grants and the same treatment as white Loyalists. In addition, another 3,000 black slaves came to Canada as servants and labourers with their white loyalist masters.

Birchtown, Nova Scotia

A new town, Birchtown, Nova Scotia, became the centre for free black Loyalists and the largest black communities in North America. Some of the black Loyalists did not receive the land grants they had been promised; however, others did. Stephen Blucke, a leading black citizen and colonel in the militia, became the largest landowner in Birchtown.

Freedom was new to many of the blacks, who turned to churches, schools, and family for support in their new communities. Evangelistic preachers such as Joseph Leonard, Cato Perkins, Blind Moses Wilkinson, and Boston King emerged to lead the people. David George, a former slave, had started the Silver Bluff Baptist Church in South Carolina — the first black congregation in North America. In Nova Scotia, he continued preaching as a black Loyalist. Hector Peters became an evangelist in Nova Scotia and later, the first Baptist missionary in Sierra Leone in West Africa.

Back to Africa

Disappointed by broken promises and the harsh, cold Canadian life, many black Loyalists in Nova Scotia united behind Thomas Peters. Peters, a former slave from North Carolina, had fought during the American Revolution as a sergeant with the Black Pioneers. He took the demands of the unhappy black Loyalists to England. Although half had been born in North America, they all wanted to go back to Africa.

In 1792, they were granted free passage by the British government to the colony of Sierra Leone, established by black Loyalists from England in 1787. About 1,200, one third of the black Loyalists in Nova Scotia, followed their leaders to Sierra Leone. Fifteen ships loaded with 734 adults and 456 children left Halifax; 65 people died during the rough sea voyage. When the survivors arrived in Africa, they built Freetown. It became the largest West African coastal city.

Loyal to Canada

The two thirds of the black Loyalists who remained in Canada became productive citizens. Many were given land claims and became successful farmers. As slaves on the American plantations, some had learned trades such as those of: blacksmith, boatbuilder, carpenter, caulker, cooper, lumberman, mason, millwright, and sawyer. Others had skills that allowed them to become cooks, domestics, gardeners, liverymen, nursemaids, seamstresses, and tavern workers. Although many of the strong leaders of the community went to Africa, others, such as Stephen Blucke, the largest landowner in Birchtown, opposed the exodus. They stayed in Canada.

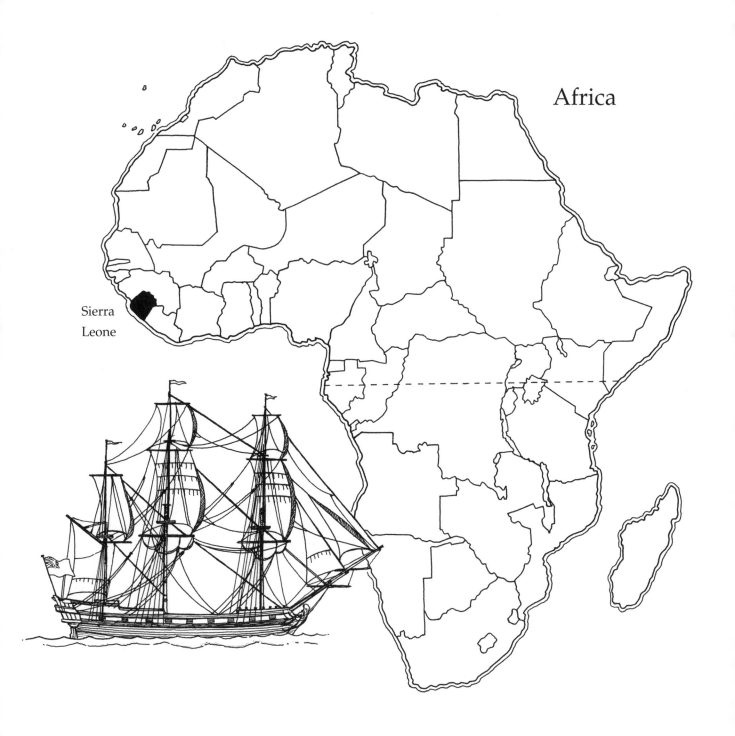

Africa

Sierra
Leone

Loyal Canadians

In 1837, when William Lyon Mackenzie and his followers revolted* and set up a Canadian provisional government on Navy Island, nearly 1,000 blacks joined the loyal militia that defeated his army. In the USA, slavery was still legal and they feared that they might lose their freedom if Mackenzie was successful in overthrowing the Canadian government.

White Race Riots

In Nova Scotia, many blacks became sharecroppers, hired labourers, or servants. Bad conditions led to rivalry with poor whites and in July of 1784, a race riot broke out in Shelburne and Birchtown that lasted for 10 days, until Governor Parr sent the army and navy to restore order.

Underground Railway

For many years, Upper Canada (Ontario), became the final stop in the secret "underground railway" that helped to smuggle thousands of blacks escaping slavery in the USA into Canada, where slavery had been abolished since 1793. It was organized by a strong-minded black woman named Harriet Tubman, and continued to operate up until the American Civil War.

*Watch for the next book in this Discovering Canada series, *The Rebels*, for more information.

Rose Fortune

First Policewoman

There were only about 100 free black settlers in Nova Scotia, before the arrival of over 3,500 black Loyalists between 1782 and 1784. Many of the new arrivals were skilled workers; others, such as Rose Fortune, created their own business opportunities. She opened a successful moving company and later became North America's first policewoman.

End of Slavery

On July 9, 1793, John Graves Simcoe convinced the Upper Canadian Assembly to pass an act that outlawed slavery. Slavery was phased out, and disappeared by 1820.

Although Britain offered freedom to slaves in the Canadian colonies, slavery remained legal in the British Empire until 1833 and in the United States until after the Civil War. Canada was thus the first free haven for slaves in North America.

Rebel Slave

Henry Washington, a black Loyalist who had been a slave on George Washington's plantation in Virginia, was one of the blacks who sailed from Nova

Scotia to Africa. In 1800, he was part of an uprising in Sierra Leone that attempted to establish independence but, unlike George's rebellion, Henry's failed and he was banished from the colony.

Slavery in Canada

Slavery was abolished in 1793 in Upper Canada, but it took until 1820 to phase it out. It was common for people to own slaves in the late 1700s and early 1800s. Many Loyalists brought their slaves with them when they settled here after the American Revolution. Joseph Brant, the Mohawk chief, owned several, as did Laura Secord, who became famous in the War of 1812.

Crossword Puzzle

ACROSS:

3   Canada was the first country to abolish this custom or practice.

4   The British general who arrived at New York with an army of 24,000 troops in July of 1776.

6   The man who received this new title of Lord and who convinced the British government to divide Canada into Upper Canada and Lower Canada.

7   The commanding officer of loyal guerrillas from North and South Carolina.

12   The name of an act passed by the British government in 1774 that created Canada, which at this time included the present day states of Michigan, Wisconsin, Illinois, Ohio, and Indiana.

15   Tenant farmers in French-speaking Canada.

16   The Royal Proclamation in 1763 declared that this mountain range would be the border between American settlers and native tribes.

17   The governor of Nova Scotia who had to deal with mass migration of Loyalists from the USA in 1783.

19   A loyal native chief who settled with is tribe in Upper Canada after the revolution.

21   The rebel city that became famous for a "Tea Party" in 1773.

22   The general in command of all British forces at the end of the revolution who was responsible for evacuation the Loyalists from the USA in 1783.

24   The British lost 13 of these during the American Revolution.

25   The governor of Canada who had to deal with the mass migration of Loyalists from the USA in 1783.

26   The commander of the loyalist force known as the King's Royal Regiment of New York.

27   The British genera whose surrender at York town in 1781 brought about the end of the war.

DOWN:

1.   Natives who were loyal allies to the king.

2   The leader of a loyalist Ranger force that settled at Niagara-on-the-Lake in 1783.

3   Loyalist who were largely responsible for successfully defending the fortress at Quebec.

5   The man who wrote the American Declaration of Independence.

8   The new political body that created the Continental Army in 1775 and declared independence from Britain in 1776.

9   About one third of the black Loyalist who come to Nova Scotia sailed to this place in 1792.

10   Elite landowners in French-speaking Canada.

11   Another name of an American "Patriot" in 1776.

13   The general who was placed in command of the rebel Continental Army in 1775.

14   Another name for a British "tory" in 1776.

18   The first country to join the American Rebels by declaring war against Britain.

20   Loyal French-speaking businesses in Canada.

23   The sister of Joseph Brant who married a powerful white landowner in the Mohawk Valley.

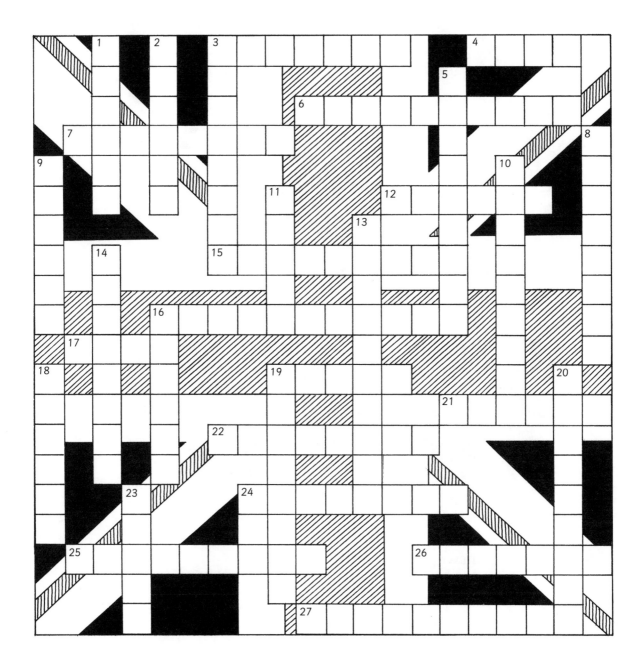

LOYALIST CROSSWORD PUZZLE ANSWERS

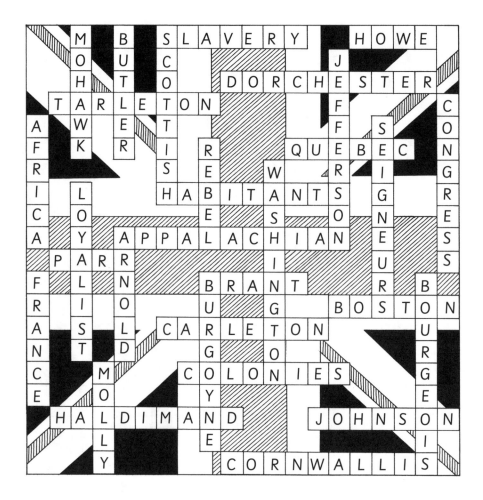

Match the Job Answers from pages 74 and 75.

1g, 2d, 3b, 4c, 5a, 6h, 7j, 8i, 9e, 10f

Index